Bible Codecrackers:
Jesus

© Gillian Ellis 2006

First published 2006
ISBN 1 84427 207 9

Scripture Union, 207-209 Queensway, Bletchley, Milton Keynes, MK2 2EB, England
Email: info@scriptureunion.org.uk
Website: www.scriptureunion.org.uk

Scripture Union Australia: Locked Bag 2, Central Coast Business Centre,
NSW 2252 www.su.org.au

Scripture Union USA: PO Box 987, Valley Forge, PA 19482, USA
www.scriptureunion.org

All rights reserved. No part of this publication may be reproduced, stored in a
retrieval system or transmitted in any form or by any means, electronic,
mechanical, photocopying, recording or otherwise, without the prior permission of
Scripture Union.

The right of Gillian Ellis to be identified as author of this work has been asserted by
her in accordance with the Copyright, Designs and Patents Act 1988.

British Library Cataloguing in Publication Data
A catalogue record of this book is available from the British Library.

Cover design by Paul Airy (4-9-0)
Internal design and layout by Richard Jefferson
Illustrations by Pauline Adams
Printed and bound in Great Britain by Henry Ling, Dorchester

✎ Scripture Union is an international Christian charity working with churches in
more than 130 countries providing resources to bring the good news about Jesus
Christ to children, young people and families – and to encourage them to develop
spiritually through the Bible and prayer.

As well as our network of volunteers, staff and associates who run holidays, church-
based events and school Christian groups, we produce a wide range of publications
and support those who use our resources through training programmes.

This book is dedicated to Georgia Pennells, Poppy Egan,
Reuben Egan and Isaac Porter, who tried out the puzzles and
made helpful suggestions.

Contents

	Introduction and quiz
1	Jesus is baptised
2	Jesus preaches in Nazareth
3	Jesus speaks about repentance
4	Jesus calls four fishermen
5	Jesus turns water into wine
6	Jesus preaches in Capernaum
7	Jesus heals a man with leprosy
8	Jesus heals a paralysed man
9	Jesus upsets the Pharisees
10	Jesus chooses twelve special friends
11	Jesus speaks on the mountain
12	Jesus teaches us a special prayer
13	Jesus welcomes children
14	Jesus surprises a rich young man
15	Jesus heals a man and a boy
16	Jesus names the greatest prophet
17	Jesus with the crowds
18	Jesus feeds thousands of hungry people – twice!
19	Jesus welcomes more believers
20	Jesus brings a man back from the dead
21	Jesus returns to Jerusalem
22	Jesus teaches in the temple
23	Jesus is questioned
24	Jesus talks about the future
25	Jesus is betrayed by a so-called friend
26	Jesus eats a final meal with his friends
27	Jesus is arrested
28	Jesus is put on trial
29	Jesus is tried by the Roman governor
30	Jesus is crucified
31	Jesus is buried – and comes alive again!
32	Jesus goes back to heaven
	Quiz and puzzle answers

Introduction

We read in the Bible about the crowds who followed Jesus everywhere during the three years he spent spreading the word of God. Those crowds thought Jesus was really something – until he found himself in trouble with the men in authority. Then some of them turned against him – but not everyone. You are about to meet one young man, aged 13, who watched what Jesus did and came to believe in him. He did not really exist, but, seeing Jesus' amazing acts through his eyes will help us to see and understand Jesus ourselves.

Oh, and while you're about it, tackle some puzzles to help you remember the great things Jesus did and said. Have fun!

Are you on your toes? Solve the puzzles and read the bible passages to answer this quiz. You can find the answers at the back of the book. Good hunting!

Quiz

1   What rested on Jesus after his baptism?
2   What does a prophet not have in his own country?
3   Name the fishermen whom Jesus helped in the story?
4   What did Jesus say he would make the four friends into?
5   How many water jars were there at the wedding in Cana?
6   Which disciple was especially grateful to Jesus?
7   What did the man with leprosy do after he was healed?
8   What did Jesus tell the lame man to do?
9   In which building did Jesus meet the man with the withered hand?
10   What is the last horizontal name in the word search?
11   What will happen to the pure in heart?
12   What did Jesus tell us always to look for?
13   What did Jesus say belonged to little children?
14   What animal does Jesus mention in this story?
15   What was worrying the Roman soldier?
16   Why was God sending his messenger?
17   What was the name of Herod's wife?
18   How many people were in the first crowd Jesus fed?
19   What was the name of the blind man healed by Jesus?
20   Where did Jesus go to be safe?
21   What two things did the people throw in Jesus' path?
22   What did Jesus say the temple was being used as?
23   The commandments say we must love God – and who else?
24   What festival did Jesus say it would be in two days' time?
25   What reward was Judas offered for betraying Jesus?
26   What food and drink did Jesus use as symbols at the Passover Feast?
27   Which of Jesus' special friends didn't run away on his arrest?
28   What vital question was Jesus asked?
29   Which criminal did Pontius Pilate release at Passover?
30   How many others were crucified with Jesus?
31   When Mary met Jesus at the tomb, who did she think he was?
32   How will Jesus come back to earth?

1
Jesus is baptised

My mum told me not to go – but I went anyway. I'm 13. I'm discovering what I can and can't do.

Some people thought it was dangerous to have anything to do with the preacher called John. He looked wild, it's true – but I felt excited and jumpy inside when I heard him speak.

"Repent of your sins!" John shouted to anyone who'd listen. "Let God wash them away! I will baptise you in his name with the water in the river."

A man standing nearby told me that my "sins" were all the wrong things I'd done. Too many to count, I thought sadly. Was it true? Could God wash my sins away, make me clean again? What an offer!

I felt fantastic after John had pushed me down into the water of the River Jordan. Just as I scrambled back on the bank, a hush fell. A stranger was kneeling alone before John, right there in the water. But John didn't want to baptise him. He seemed to know the man. He called him "Jesus".

"*You* should baptise *me*!" said John, but the man shook his head.

"We must do everything right," he answered quietly. So John baptised him.

You'll never guess what happened next!

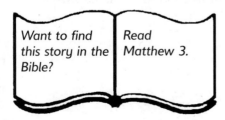

Want to find this story in the Bible? Read Matthew 3.

	1	2	3	4	5	6	7	8	9	10

Write the letters downwards in the grid under the appropriate number to find out what happened next.

1	T R N O A H T L M E
2	H I L N V E H O W D
3	E T I J O A I V E W
4	H C K E I V S E L I
5	O A E S C E I D L T
6	L M A U E N S S P H
7	Y E D S F S M O L H
8	S D O A R A Y N E I
9	P O V N O I B I A M
10	I W E D M D E A S !

2

Jesus preaches in Nazareth

When I heard Jesus was teaching at Nazareth, I couldn't get there fast enough. He was the most amazing preacher. His face lit up when he talked and I loved the way he called God his Father, just as though he really knew him well. Some of the local Jewish leaders grumbled afterwards.

"Who does he think he is?" they muttered. "He's only Mary and Joseph's boy – what makes him think he can tell us what to do?"

Jesus had an answer for them, of course. You can read about this in Matthew 13:53–58.

Sort this list of words into the right order, following the number message.

1.	A	7.	HONOUR	12.	NOT
2.	ACCEPTABLE	8.	HOUSE	13.	OFTEN
3.	AND	9.	IN	14.	OWN
4.	COUNTRY	10.	IS	15.	PROPHET
5.	HE	11.	LAND	16.	WITHOUT
6.	HIS				

MESSAGE: 1 15 10 13 16 7 9 6 14 8 3 9 6 14 4 5 10 12 2 9 6 14 11

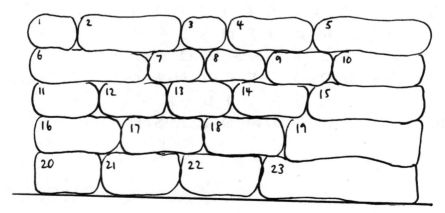

3

Jesus speaks about repentance

Word went around that Jesus was preaching by Lake Galilee, so I asked my mum for some bread and a water flask.

I followed Jesus and a crowd of others to Capernaum where Jesus began to preach. He used that word "repentance" again, as John had.

"Repent, for the kingdom of heaven is near!" Jesus told the people. They didn't understand, any more than I did. The only kingdom I knew about was the one we were in, ruled by the Romans who made our lives a misery most of the time.

Jesus went down to the beach where some fishermen were messing about with nets. I watched him talking to two of them and then saw him climb into a boat.

"What's he up to now?" I wondered aloud. A man standing nearby knew the two men. As the boats cast off from the shore, he told me their names.

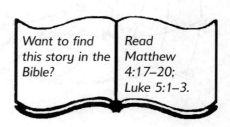

Want to find this story in the Bible? Read Matthew 4:17–20; Luke 5:1–3.

Solve this riddle to find out the two names.

My first is in mackerel, also in roach;
My second is in salmon and isn't in poach.
My third is in haddock and also in dab;
My fourth is in crayfish and also in crab.
My fifth is in oyster, encased in its shell;
My sixth is in whitebait - and whiting, as well.
My seventh's in sprat (and it starts a new name);
My eighth is in herring (and kipper – the same).
My ninth is in monkfish, in shrimp and in bream;
My tenth is in sturgeon – its roe is supreme!
Eleventh's in tuna but isn't in trout;
Now both of the brothers are named – work it out!

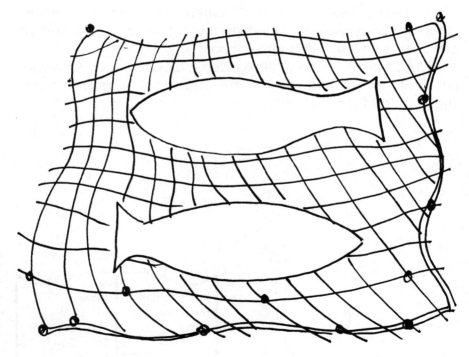

Write their names in the net.

4
Jesus calls four fishermen

Jesus rowed away with the two fishermen and then he stood up in the boat. From there Jesus spoke to the crowds on the beach. It wasn't like it had been in Nazareth – these people really wanted to hear what Jesus had to say.

Then I heard Jesus telling Simon and Andrew to row further out and throw their nets into the water. His words carried clearly through the still air. The man next to me gave a grunt.

"Do them no good," he said, gruffly. "We've been trying all night and not caught so much as a sprat. Waste of time."

The men rowed out and cast their nets. Next minute they were struggling frantically, hauling on the nets as the boat rocked wildly.

"James! John!" they yelled. "We need some help. Give us a hand!" The man next to me and another man ran to the water, jumped in a boat and rowed madly towards their friends. The four fishermen hauled hundreds of fish into the two boats. They had great difficulty rowing back to the beach. The boats were overflowing.

I expected them to pile their fish on carts to take them to market. But Jesus spoke to them. They left the piles of fish and simply walked away!

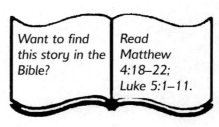

Want to find this story in the Bible? Read Matthew 4:18–22; Luke 5:1–11.

Whatever could he have said to make them do that? The answer is in this peculiar picture story.

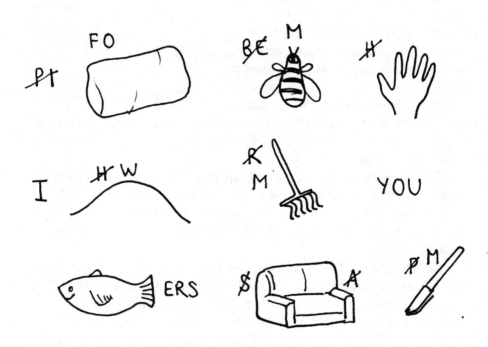

Write the answer text here:

"_ _ _ _ _ _ _ / _ _ / _ _ _ _ / _ / _ _ _ _ /

_ _ _ _ / _ _ _ / _ _ _ _ _ _ _ _ / _ _ / _ _ _ ."

5

Jesus turns water into wine

It's not often I go to a wedding but my cousin was marrying a girl in Cana and our whole family was invited. It was a very smart occasion, which surprised me because our family isn't all that well off. But my mum said her sister liked to do things properly, even if they couldn't afford it.

I was thrilled to find Jesus there with his mum. The music and dancing were great and the wine flowed – well, it flowed for most of the time. Then – disaster – it ran out. My aunt was really upset.

"What will people think of us?" my aunt whispered, tears streaming down her face. "We'll be disgraced in front of all our friends."

Mary, Jesus' mum, overheard what she said.

"Don't worry," she said. "I'll have a word with my son. He'll sort it out."

I heard Jesus tell some servants to fill some large stone jugs with water.

"What good will that do?" said my dad, scornfully. "It's wine we need, not water. Who wants *water* at a wedding?"

"Just you wait!" I told him, but I secretly wondered why I felt so confident.

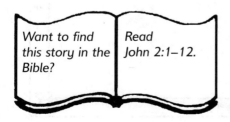

Want to find this story in the Bible? Read John 2:1–12.

Here is a jigsaw picture of the wedding at Cana – but three of the pieces don't belong. Can you tell which they are? You may like to draw the wedding in the photo frame to help you or photocopy this page.

6

Jesus preaches in Capernaum

Jesus was pretty popular in Capernaum and he often went there. I went with him whenever I could, and my mum and dad even came with me after my cousin's wedding.

One time, when Jesus was preaching in the Capernaum synagogue, I spotted the four fishermen who were his special friends. Everything was going well when suddenly there was a disturbance. A crazy-looking man rushed into the synagogue and yelled at Jesus, "Why are you here? Have you come to destroy us, Jesus of Nazareth?"

Jesus answered sternly, "Be silent and come out!" The man screamed and started to shake – then suddenly, everything was calm.

People began to whisper. "The rabbi has driven an evil spirit out of him. What's happening? Is this a new teaching? This man even has an authority over evil spirits – see how they obey him!" Everyone was amazed at what Jesus had done.

Jesus healed many people in Capernaum. Some were ill, others lame, blind or deaf. Some, like the man in the synagogue, had "evil spirits" in them who were messing about with their minds.

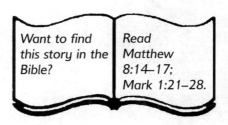

| Want to find this story in the Bible? | Read Matthew 8:14–17; Mark 1:21–28. |

One of Jesus' special friends was especially grateful to him. Fill in the missing vowels to find out why. Start at the arrow.

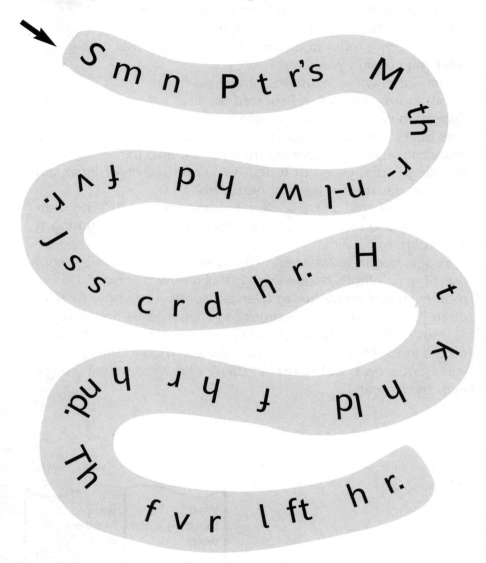

7

Jesus heals a man with leprosy

Leprosy is a terrible disease and my mum won't let me go near anyone who has it. I don't know if it's catching or not but she won't take a chance. Anyone with leprosy has to wear a little bell so that people hear them coming.

Several of us were listening to the teacher one day when we heard that familiar little bell. We all scattered – all except Jesus. The man came right up to him and knelt on the ground.

"Master," he said, gazing anxiously at Jesus, "if you choose, you can make me well." Jesus immediately touched the man and said, "I will. Be clean."

Right before our eyes, the horrible white scabby scales melted away and the man's skin became smooth. He leapt up with a big grin on his face. He was ready to shout his thanks to the world – but Jesus stopped him. By now, we were all staring with wonder at the man's skin. We heard Jesus say softly, "Don't tell anyone what's happened. Go to the priest and make a thank-offering to God as Moses commanded."

The man clasped Jesus' hands. He was so grateful. He went to do what Jesus had said.

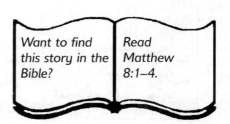

Want to find this story in the Bible? Read Matthew 8:1–4.

How many differences can you spot here?

8

Jesus heals a paralysed man

Lots of people had crowded into a house where Jesus was preaching. I overslept that morning and had to run all the way, but I was too late. I was furious that I had to stay outside the house. There was no room inside. Now I wouldn't hear what the teacher was saying!

But as things turned out, I was in the best place to see what happened next. Four men arrived with a man on a stretcher; he was unable to walk. They'd heard that Jesus could heal people so brought their friend to him. But the house was so full; they couldn't think how to get the man inside. Then I had a brainwave.

"Why not take the stretcher up on the roof and let it down through a hole?" I suggested, rather pleased with my own brilliance. "You'd only need to shift a few planks, then lower it on a rope..." One man ran home for a rope and the friends set to work. They cut a hole in the roof and, with much puffing and panting, lowered the stretcher through the hole. I peered down through the hole. I didn't expect to hear or see what I did...

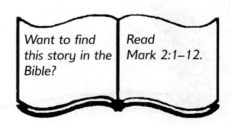

Want to find this story in the Bible? Read Mark 2:1–12.

You can read what happened on our story wheel. Start with the letter in the centre; then read the letters in the wheel in clockwise order, starting at the middle circle and working outwards. Write down the letters as you go. Always start the next circle by reading the letter to the right of the bold line first.

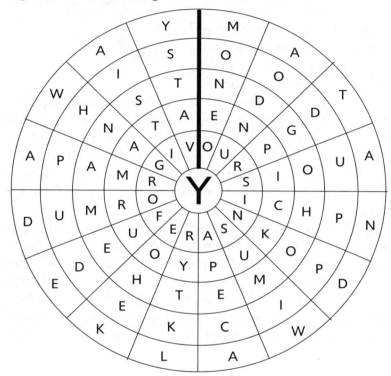

Write the story on the mat

9

Jesus upsets the Pharisees

We all knew the rules about working on the Sabbath, the Jewish holy day. From when we were very young, we'd been taught that God had blessed the seventh day of the week and told us to keep it as a day of rest. So I suppose it should have felt odd when we saw Jesus healing on the Sabbath. But strangely enough, it didn't. It seemed perfectly natural.

The Pharisees were the religious leaders who insisted we kept every part of the law. They kicked up an awful fuss when Jesus let his hungry disciples pick bits of grain to eat on the Sabbath. That's how strict our Jewish law is.

Jesus spoke to them and said, "Remember King David all those years ago? He and his men were hungry so they ate the temple bread that only the priests were supposed to eat. They didn't do wrong. The Sabbath was made for man, not the other way round. I am Lord of the Sabbath – it doesn't rule me."

There were other times when Jesus "worked" on the Sabbath and upset those Pharisees. It got so bad that some of them decided to get rid of him.

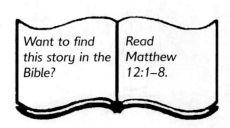

Want to find this story in the Bible? Read Matthew 12:1–8.

Which two Pharisees are the same in the pictures below?

22

10

Jesus chooses twelve special friends

After I saw that paralysed man walk out of the house, I followed Jesus all over the region of Galilee. I saw him heal loads of sick people. One evening, Jesus went on his own to the hills. He wanted to pray, he said. He prayed all night. In the morning, we found out what he'd been praying about. He'd been asking God to help him make a very important decision.

He was choosing some men to be his special team. He called them "apostles" – Dad told me an apostle is a messenger, someone who's sent on a mission.

Jesus chose twelve men, all very different. You can read this in Matthew 10:1–4.

Here's a verse to help you remember them – and a puzzle, of course...

There was **Simon**, there was **Andrew**; they were brothers by the sea.
There was **James** and there was **John**; they were the sons of Zebedee.
They were glad to go with Jesus as he walked along the shore;
So they left their nets and went with him to look for several more.
They spotted **Matthew** sitting at his tax collector's seat;
So Jesus had a chat and even stayed with him to eat.
Bartholomew and **Philip** joined the eager band of men;
Then **Simon**, **James** and **Judas** brought the number up to ten.
But Jesus wanted twelve good men to spread the word abroad;
So **Thaddaeus** and **Thomas** joined the followers of the Lord.

See if you can find the 12 apostles' names in this word search. You will also find the names **Zebedee**, **Zealot**, **Alphaeus** and **Iscariot**. As you find each name, cross it out, and then write down the remaining letters in order to read what Jesus is doing in this story.

Z	E	B	E	D	E	E	J	E	S	U
E	S	A	N	D	R	E	W	C	A	L
A	L	R	S	T	H	E	M	T	J	I
L	W	T	H	A	D	D	A	E	U	S
O	T	H	O	M	A	S	T	P	D	C
T	J	O	H	N	J	S	T	H	A	A
S	A	L	E	L	A	I	H	I	S	R
I	M	O	V	E	M	M	E	L	D	I
M	E	M	I	S	E	O	W	I	C	O
O	S	E	I	P	S	N	L	P	E	T
N	S	W	A	L	P	H	A	E	U	S

_ _ _ _ _ / _ _ _ _ _ _ / _ _ _ / _ _ _ _ _ _ _ / _ _ _ _ _ _ _ _

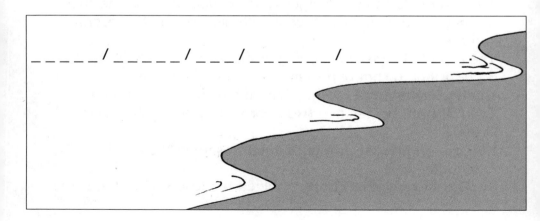

24

11

Jesus speaks on the mountain

Jesus gave his special friends God's power to heal all kinds of illnesses and to cast out evil spirits. He took them all over the countryside, followed by a great crowd – including me, of course. People came from miles around to hear him, even from the other side of the River Jordan.

Jesus started by saying that God blesses us all in different ways. They call his words "the beatitudes", which means "the blessings". Here are some of them.

See if you can work out what Jesus said from these mixed up words.

"Blessed are the ROPO NI TRIPSI, _ _ _ _ / _ _ / _ _ _ _ _ _ _ ,

for theirs is the kingdom of NEAVEH. _ _ _ _ _ _ _ .

Blessed are the KEME, _ _ _ _ _ ,

for they shall inherit the RETHA. _ _ _ _ _ _ .

Blessed are the LUFCRIME, _ _ _ _ _ _ _ _ ,

for they shall receive CRYME. _ _ _ _ _ _ .

Blessed are the ERUP NI THEAR, _ _ _ _ /_ _ / _ _ _ _ _ _ ,

for they shall EES DGO." _ _ _ / _ _ _ ."

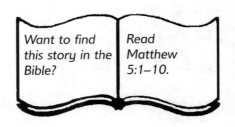

Want to find this story in the Bible? Read Matthew 5:1–10.

12

Jesus teaches us a special prayer

Jesus said so many things it's hard to remember them all – but I'll try, because what he taught us was so important. He told his disciples that they were the salt of the earth and the light of the world.

Jesus told us not to show off, to do good deeds and to pray in secret. He taught us a new prayer.

> *Our Father in heaven:*
> *May your holy name be honoured;*
> *May your kingdom come;*
> *May your will be done on earth as it is in heaven.*
> *Give us today the food we need.*
> *Forgive us the wrongs we have done,*
> *As we forgive the wrongs that others have done to us.*
> *Do not bring us to hard testing,*
> *But keep us safe from the Evil One.*

Jesus finished with a story about some builders: a wise one who built his house on a rock and a foolish one who built on sand. When it began to rain heavily, the wise man's house stood firm and the foolish man's house collapsed.

One important thing sticks in my mind. He told us not to worry about problems we might have but to look for something very special.

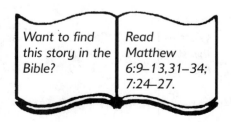

Want to find this story in the Bible? Read Matthew 6:9–13, 31–34; 7:24–27.

Read this picture message to find out what it was.

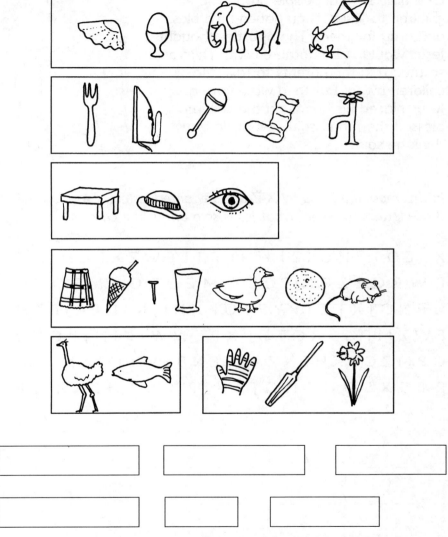

To find the "something special", write down the initial letter of each object shown in the boxes above – one word is in each box.

27

13

Jesus welcomes children

One time several people brought their children to Jesus. They hoped he'd bless and pray for them. The apostles thought Jesus wouldn't be bothered with children so they told the parents to take the children away. But they were wrong. Jesus placed his hands on the children, blessed them and said... what do you think he said?

In this message J P Q W X Z are unwanted letters. Cross out all those letters to reveal what Jesus said about the children.

X L E Q T T H E X Z L I T J P P T L E W Z X P C H J I L J
D W R Q E Z P N Z C O Q M E Q T O X M E Q Z D
O P N O J X T Z T R Y P T O P X H I J N J D E R J P T H
E W Z M F O X R Q T H P X P E W W J K I N J P G X D
O P M Z O F X H E X Z A J V E N B E W L O J X N G S Z
P T O X S Q U C H Q J A S J P X W T H E S X W E

"_ _ _ / _ _ _ / _ _ _ _ _ _ / _ _ _ _ _ _ _ _ / _ _ _ _ / _ _ / _ _.

_ _ / _ _ _ / _ _ _ / _ _ / _ _ _ _ _ _ _ / _ _ _ _ / _ _ _ / _ _ _ /

_ _ _ _ _ _ _ / _ _ / _ _ _ _ _ _ / _ _ _ _ _ _ _ / _ _ / _ _ _ _ /

_ _ / _ _ _ _ _ _."

Want to find this story in the Bible? Read Matthew 19:13–15.

14

Jesus surprises a rich young man

Jesus often said things that puzzled people. A young man came to him and asked, "I want to do something really good to make sure I go to heaven. What can that be?"

Jesus answered, "Only God is good. But you know the commandments – keep them."

"But shouldn't I do something more than that?" asked the young man, eagerly.

"If you want to be perfect," said Jesus, "sell everything you own, give the money away to the poor and then follow me. Your reward will be in heaven."

The young man was very rich. It was just too hard for him to give everything away. He went away very sad.

Jesus then said something that made his followers wonder who could go to heaven. Work out what it is.

Write down the letters in the squares in the order 1,2,3,4 to find out the strange thing Jesus said. Do the first square first, then the next and so on.

1 2
4 3

I	T	E	A	E	R	R	A	M	E	O	G	H	R	G	H	E	E	O	F	E	E
S	I	I	S	O	F	A	C	T	L	T	O	U	O	H	T	E	Y	N	A	L	D

E	T	N	F	A	R	H	M	T	O	T	E	H	E	N	G	M	O	O	D
A	H	R	O	C	I	N	A	N	E	T	R	I	K	O	D	G	F	*	*

"_ _ / _ _ / _ _ _ _ _ _ / _ _ _ / _ / _ _ _ _ _ / _ _ / _ _ /
_ _ _ _ _ _ / _ _ _ / _ _ _ / _ _ / _ / _ _ _ _ _ _ / _ _ _ _ /
_ _ _ / _ / _ _ _ _ / _ _ _ / _ _ / _ _ _ _ _ _ / _ _ _ /
_ _ _ _ _ _ / _ _ / _ _ _."

Want to find this story in the Bible? Read Matthew 19:16–26.

29

15

Jesus heals a man and a boy

One day I was with Jesus as he entered Capernaum. A Roman soldier ran up and spoke urgently to Jesus. I was close enough to hear what he 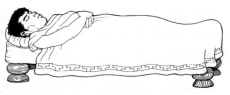 said. (On the next page, you'll find the conversation I heard. Use the key to help you work it out.) One thing I will tell you - Jesus didn't even need to go to the soldier's house. He just did what the soldier asked.

Just as Jesus was going through the gates of a town called Nain, we came across a funeral procession. One of the mourners told us the dead man was the only son of a widow. She was weeping as she followed her son's body.

Jesus spoke gently to the widow. "Don't cry." He touched the stretcher the body lay on. Everyone gasped as the man sat up, alive again! His mother flung her arms around him, almost unable to believe this wonderful miracle. Two amazing healings in one day!

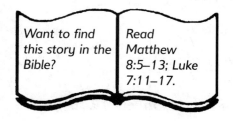

Want to find this story in the Bible?

Read Matthew 8:5–13; Luke 7:11–17.

To find out what I heard, you'll need this number code.

Z Y X W V U T S R Q P O N M L K J I H G F E D C B A
1 2 3 4 5 6 7 8 9 10 11 12 13 14 15 16 17 18 19 20 21 22 23 24 25 26

Roman:

15 12 9 23 / 14 2 / 8 22 9 5 26 13 7 / 18 8 /
26 7 / 19 12 14 22 / 5 22 9 2 / 18 15 15.

"_ _ _ _, / _ _ / _ _ _ _ _ _ _ / _ _ /
_ _ / _ _ _ _, / _ _ _ _ / _ _ _."

Jesus:

18 / 4 18 15 15 / 20 12 / 26 13 23 / 19 22 26 15 / 19 18 14.

"_ / _ _ _ _ / _ _ / _ _ _ / _ _ _ _ / _ _ _."

Roman:

17 6 8 7 / 8 26 2 / 7 19 22 / 4 12 9 23 / 26 13 23 / 14 2 /
8 22 9 5 26 13 7 / 4 18 15 15 / 25 22 / 19 22 26 15 22 23.

"_ _ _ _ / _ _ _ / _ _ _ / _ _ _ _ / _ _ _ / _ _ /
_ _ _ _ _ _ _ / _ _ _ _ / _ _ / _ _ _ _ _ _."

Jesus:

18 / 19 26 5 22 / 13 12 7 / 21 12 6 13 23 / 26 13 2 12 13 22 /
18 13 / 18 8 9 26 22 15 / 4 18 7 19 / 8 6 24 19 /
20 9 22 26 7 / 21 26 18 7 19.

"_ / _ _ _ _ / _ _ _ / _ _ _ _ _ _ / _ _ _ _ _ _ _ /
_ _ / _ _ _ _ _ _ _ / _ _ _ _ / _ _ _ _ /
_ _ _ _ _ / _ _ _ _ _."

16

Jesus names the greatest prophet

News of all the fantastic things Jesus was doing spread like wildfire. More and more people followed him everywhere. He healed many people and taught about the kingdom of God.

One day, two men came to see him. They were friends of Jesus' cousin John, who had baptised Jesus in the River Jordan. When they saw Jesus do such wonderful things they said, "John sent us to ask if you are the promised Messiah or are we to wait for someone else?"

Jesus replied, "Tell John what you've seen and heard. Blind people see, lame people walk, deaf people hear, dead people live again and lepers are cleansed." When John's friends had left, Jesus spoke to us about John.

Solve this puzzle by looking back to find out what Jesus said about him.

"TSITPAB EHT NHOJ NAHT TEHPORP RETAERG ON SI EREHT YAS I"

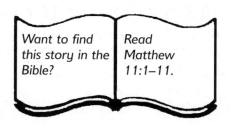

Want to find this story in the Bible? Read Matthew 11:1–11.

17

Jesus with the crowds

Over the next three years, my friends and I followed Jesus and his special friends whenever we could. I was almost 16 by then.

During that time, the ruler of Galilee, King Herod, heard about Jesus and was very puzzled about him. He kept asking if Jesus was John the Baptist come back to life. That really worried him. You see, a couple of years earlier, he'd had John killed. Solve the puzzle to find out why he'd murdered John.

Here's the puzzle. All the vowels are missing from these sentences. Put them back in to find out why John the Baptist was killed.

H*R*D H*D M*RR**D H*S BR*TH*R'S W*F*
H*R*D**S. J*HN S**D TH*T TH*S W*S WR*NG.
H*R*D**S W*S *NGRY *ND W*TH TH* H*LP
*F H*R D**GHT*R S*L*M*, TR*CK*D H*R*D
NT PR*M*S*NG T* K*LL J*HN.

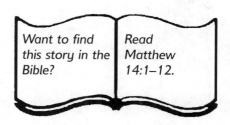

Want to find this story in the Bible? Read Matthew 14:1–12.

33

18

Jesus feeds thousands of hungry people – twice!

Jesus had been talking to a crowd of people all day. We were starving hungry. The apostles thought we should go and find our own food in the nearest village, but Jesus said, "Give them something to eat here."

That sounded a bit odd because the only food anyone had was five loaves and a couple of fish. That would feed a few people – but there must have been well over **5,000** of us!

Jesus told us all to sit down on the grass. He looked up to heaven and picked up the five loaves and two small fish. He thanked God for them, broke them into pieces and handed the pieces to the apostles, telling them to give the food to us.

They started handing out bits of bread and fish – and it just went on forever. **Five** loaves and **two** small fish fed this huge crowd.

When everyone had had enough, the apostles went round and filled **12** baskets with the crumbs of food left on the ground.

A few weeks later, the same thing happened again. This time, after speaking for **three** days, Jesus fed over **4,000** people with **seven** loaves and a few fish – and there were **seven** baskets of leftovers!

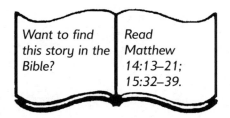

| Want to find this story in the Bible? | Read Matthew 14:13–21; 15:32–39. |

Do you like maths? Try this sum for a bit of fun.

Sum 1 Add up the number of people in the first crowd, the number of loaves, the number of fish and the number of baskets full of leftovers.

Sum 2 Add up the number of people in the second crowd, the number of days they had been listening to Jesus, the number of loaves and the number of baskets full of leftovers.

Now take answer number 2 from answer number 1 and write your answer here.

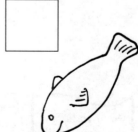

35

19

Jesus welcomes more believers

Jesus' friends had been in a boat when a great storm started blowing. They were having a hard time staying upright. Suddenly Jesus appeared walking across the waves to them. As soon as he reached the boat, the storm died down.

Jesus travelled to many different places, teaching and healing wherever he went. Sometimes he went off by himself to be quiet so he could pray. Sometimes, his special friends went with him. Whenever he returned from these days off, I was always waiting for him. I saw Jesus heal a boy with epilepsy and help a blind man in Jericho to see again. Find out the blind man's name by solving the next puzzle.

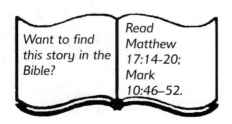

Want to find this story in the Bible? Read Matthew 17:14-20; Mark 10:46–52.

Choose from these answers and write down the word you choose in the box. Now read the initial letters downwards to find out the blind man's name.

1 Jesus healed a (young, blind, happy) man in Jericho.

2 Jesus' special friends were called (epistles, parables, apostles).

3 When the storm started, the apostles were (sewing, eating, rowing).

4 After the storm, Jesus travelled to (Tyre, Rome, Bath).

5 One of Jesus' friends was called Judas (Ferguson, Iscariot, Williams).

6 Jesus' mother was named (Anna, Jane, Mary).

7 Simon Peter's brother was named (Andrew, Joseph, Reuben).

8 The second book of the Bible is called (Isaiah, Exodus, Judges).

9 Passover bread is called (overheated, overcooked, unleavened).

10 The Jews' special day of rest is called the (Missive, Festive, Sabbath).

37

20

Jesus brings a man back from the dead

Lazarus, the brother of Mary and Martha, was a friend of Jesus. He had fallen ill and died. He had been dead four days and was wrapped in cloth and put inside a tomb. Bound to be smelly. Jesus stood outside the tomb and called his name. Lazarus just walked out of the tomb, still wrapped in his burial clothes. I could hardly believe my eyes!

That *really* convinced people that Jesus was the promised Messiah, God's own son. But some didn't believe. They went running off to tell the Pharisees what they'd seen.

The chief priests and the Pharisees called a gathering of the Sanhedrin, the Jewish Council, to discuss what to do about Jesus. It was clear they were out to get him. From then on, it wasn't safe for Jesus and his special friends to walk openly in the streets and towns. Instead, they went out into the country to a place called... work it out.

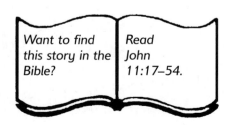

| Want to find this story in the Bible? | Read John 11:17–54. |

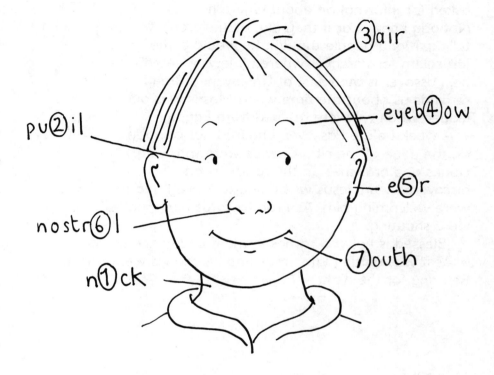

Write the missing letters in the grid. The numbers show you where to put them.

Jesus went for safety to

1	2	3	4	5	6	7

21

Jesus returns to Jerusalem

The Jewish Council ordered Jesus' arrest and asked for information about where he was. Nobody knew – or if they did, they weren't telling. Many people thought he would come to Jerusalem for Passover where all Jews wanted to be. Passover is the Feast of Unleavened Bread. It reminds us about the time when Moses was our leader, when we were rescued from Egypt.

A week before Passover, I heard a lot of noise on the edge of the city. Crowds were throwing cloaks and branches on the road. I soon discovered why. Jesus was riding a donkey and the crowds were welcoming him. As I ran towards him, I heard what they were shouting.

"Blessed is he who comes in the name of the Lord!"

As it was getting late, Jesus and his friends went out to Bethany for the night.

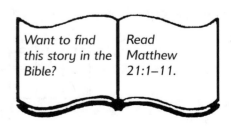

Want to find this story in the Bible? — Read Matthew 21:1–11.

Find the path Jesus took to Jerusalem.

41

22

Jesus teaches in the temple

Early next morning, I awoke just in time to hear more noise. Jesus was in the temple, hurling things about. He overturned tables and coins were rolling everywhere. Jesus was shouting – very unusual for him. Want to know what he shouted? Solve the puzzle.

Jesus was angry because the moneylenders were cheating people in the temple grounds. They changed money and sold animals and birds for sacrifices at huge prices and made lots of money for themselves. When the moneylenders had gone, Jesus began to teach. He did that every day in the temple and many people, including me, hung on his every word.

It wasn't just those who agreed with Jesus who listened carefully to what he said. The priests, scribes and elders listened, too, and asked Jesus many questions. They were trying to trap him into claiming he was the Son of God, which they thought was blasphemy. Jesus answered them very cleverly. They sent spies to trick him, but they couldn't fool Jesus.

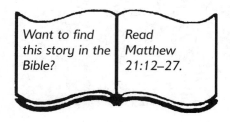

Want to find this story in the Bible? Read Matthew 21:12–27.

Cross out the first letter of the message below, then put a circle round the next letter. Now cross out the next two letters and circle the next. Next cross out three letters and circle the next, then cross out four, circle, then five, circle.

Now continue by crossing out just one letter, then two, three, four, and five as before. Go through the whole crossing out game again and again until you reach the end of the message. Write the circled letters in order in the speech bubble and it will tell you what Jesus said when he was so angry at the temple.

A "I X N T S K D I S P O T S A D H T Y W D R A L I A I T T F
W Z X T S H I W E E C N T Y 'M V N I Y W O R U H S K G H
T O A U C B S P O I E S F H Y W A S G T H I B L A S L Z X
G B M U Y E E C H E T Y C S A P O L H S K L L A H E E C N
E H T D Q A O Z H Q U T O P O W F U C H E T Y S N E M
N O A D K F Q T Y E P C O N U E R A A O O Y P O E E C V
B Z R.' O P M E Y B A U W Q T A U R Y C H U T O Z X W E
R U Q A N M R A L P E W I T Y M A P O T Y A A K A N I L
K J N H J O I G W E R T Y I B T V B A B N X D O Z X W E A
D R T Y N S O H J F C H Y R V B O U O C B N W R B U B I
T E S R E R V N E T S G I V T R !"

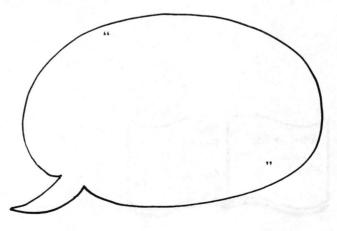

43

23

Jesus is questioned

The Jewish teachers were often questioning Jesus. The Pharisees wanted to know which was the greatest of the Ten Commandments God had given Moses. These rules had been taught us since we were very young!

Some of the commandments are quite long but here's a summary. They tell us to love and worship only God, to turn away from any man-made idols and not to use God's name as a swear word. They tell us to keep the Sabbath holy, to respect our parents, not to kill and to be faithful in marriage. They tell us not to steal anything, not to lie and not to envy other people. Of course, we have a whole long book of other laws we try to keep but those were the ones God gave Moses all those years ago.

Jesus summed up these commandments. Solve this puzzle to find out what he said.

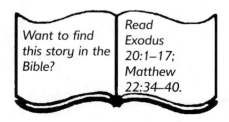

Want to find this story in the Bible?
Read Exodus 20:1–17; Matthew 22:34–40.

The words below all fit into the framework – all you have to do is to decide which word goes where. A few letters have been put in to help you discover how Jesus answered the Pharisees.

2 letters:	AS IS IS
3 letters:	ALL ALL ALL AND GOD THE THE THE YOU YOU
4 letters:	LORD LOVE LOVE MIND SOUL YOUR YOUR YOUR YOUR YOUR WITH WITH WITH
5 letters:	FIRST GREAT HEART SHALL SHALL
6 letters:	SECOND
8 letters:	YOURSELF
9 letters:	NEIGHBOUR
11 letters:	COMMANDMENT

24

Jesus talks about the future

Jesus sometimes said things it was hard to understand. He said other men would claim to be the Messiah, there would be wars, suffering, famine and earthquakes. We would all be hated or even killed because we loved him. He even said that one day, with no warning, the skies would turn black – no sun, moon or stars. Then we'd see Jesus coming on the clouds with angels to take all who love him to be with him!

He told stories about the kingdom of heaven, trying to show us what it would be like. He talked about the great day of judgement when God would separate good people from the bad. Then suddenly, he said a really shocking thing. It made me feel really ill. Solve the puzzle to find out what Jesus said.

Here's what Jesus said which shocked his listeners. The first three words are done for you. Can you work out how the code works?

I T O A S T I L E H P S O E F S I A A D H S N F A W L B H N E O E T B C U I I D N W D Y I W L B T E A S V R E T V L N T E O O M N I L E A D D V R O E R C FE.*

Write the answer on the lines below.

In two days _____

_____

| Want to find this story in the Bible? | Read Matthew 24:29–31; 26:1–2. |

25
Jesus is betrayed by a so-called friend

We all knew the Jewish leaders were muttering about Jesus being a troublemaker. We were beginning to feel very uneasy, but we couldn't really believe anyone would make up lies about him. He'd healed and comforted people, told them great stories and done good everywhere he went. They should have been thanking him, not trying to kill him.

But his enemies schemed together to find a way to arrest Jesus and have him killed.

I haven't told you the worst thing of all. The devil himself got into one of Jesus' twelve special friends and he did a truly terrible thing. Find out who and what by solving this puzzle.

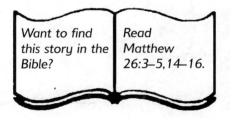

Want to find this story in the Bible? Read Matthew 26:3–5, 14–16.

Here is some pretty odd writing.

↖ ▶ ⇦ ⇨ ▽   ↓ ▽ ⇨ ⇨ △ ↓ ↕ ◀   ⇨ △ △ ⇨ ↔ → ⇨ ⇦

◀ ↕   ⇦ ⇨ ◀ △ ⇨ ▲   ↖ ⇨ ▽ ▶ ▽   ← ↕ △

◀ ↑ ↓ △ ◀ ▲   ▽ ↓ ↙ ◁ ⇨ △   ⇨ ↕ ↓ ↔ ▽.

Here is the 🗝 to decode the message.

a	b	c	d	e	f	g	h	i	j	k	l	m
⇨	⇦	⇨	⇦	⇨	←	→	↑	↓	↖	↗	↙	↘

n	o	p	q	r	s	t	u	v	w	x	y	z
↔	↕	▲	▼	△	▽	◀	▶	◁	▷	◣	◢	▼

Write the answer in the money bag.

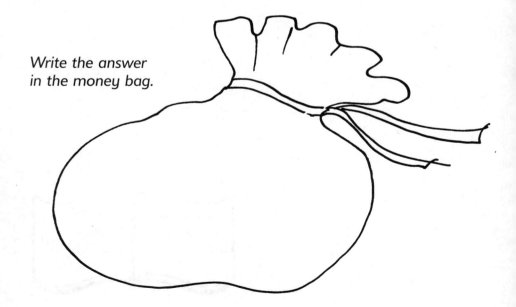

26

Jesus eats a final meal with his friends

It was the time of the Passover. Jesus had been staying in Bethany. He sent two friends into Jerusalem on the first day, to prepare the Passover Feast of Unleavened Bread. He told them to look for a man carrying a jug of water and to follow him to his house.

The man showed them an upstairs room where they could eat their meal. When they'd prepared the meal, Jesus and the others arrived. I watched them all go up the stairs.

I found out from the friends much later on what happened. Jesus thanked God and ate the food but he said a strange thing. As he broke the bread, he announced that this time, he was doing it to remind them of his body, soon to be broken. *Broken? How? Why?* The wine would represent his blood, soon to be poured out, so that God would forgive our sins.

Jesus said that one of his great friends would betray him. He also said that soon they wouldn't see him any more but that God would send someone else to comfort them. He said he'd come back later and take them to where he'd gone.

Thomas asked him where he was going. "How can we know the way?" Thomas wondered.

Want to find this story in the Bible? Read Matthew 26:17–29. John 14:1–6, 15–17.

49

Solve this puzzle to find out Jesus' answer.

Find the way to the top of the hill along the only possible path. On the way, collect the words from the signposts you pass to find out what Jesus told his friends – and us!

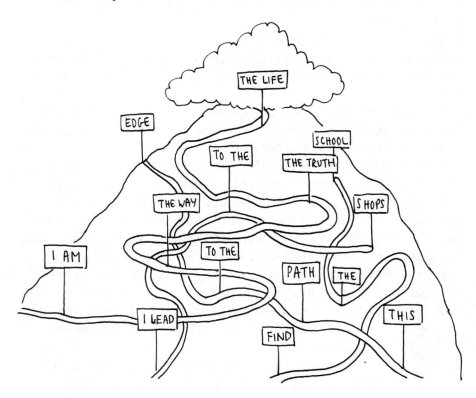

Write them on the banner.

27

Jesus is arrested

I saw Judas rush out of the house, looking very upset. Later they all came out and set off towards the Mount of Olives. I crept after them. I followed them across the brook into the Garden of Gethsemane and saw Jesus, Peter, James and John disappear into the trees further on. Everyone else settled down in the olive grove.

I fell asleep but woke suddenly. I heard tramping feet. There were lights everywhere, and a patrol of soldiers, led by Judas.

Judas went straight up to Jesus and kissed him. Immediately, the nearest soldiers seized Jesus. They had needed Judas to kiss Jesus so that in the dark they could arrest the right man. They dragged Jesus off to the high priest's house. You'll never guess what most of his special friends did. Find out by solving the puzzle.

Put the letters of each word in the right order to find out what happened. Write each correct word in a foot.

LAL ETH SPELICIDS PEEXCT MOINS PREET ARN YAWA.

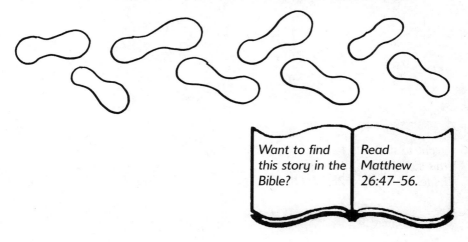

Want to find this story in the Bible? Read Matthew 26:47–56.

28

Jesus is put on trial

The high priest's house has a huge courtyard with a big high wall round it. Peter managed to sneak inside but we hung around outside, listening to what was happening. Several people told lies about Jesus. At first, the Sanhedrin couldn't make out a case against him.

Then two men said they'd heard Jesus say he would destroy the temple and rebuild it in three days. Oddly enough, they were telling the truth. He *had* said that, but he hadn't meant the Jerusalem temple. He'd been talking about the temple of his *body*. Jesus just stayed silent until Caiaphas, the high priest, asked an all-important question.

Jesus answered, "You have said so."

In Jewish law that means, "Yes, you are right." By saying that, an ordinary man would have been committing blasphemy. But Jesus was no ordinary man.

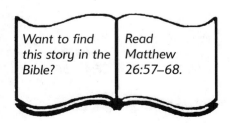

Want to find this story in the Bible? Read Matthew 26:57–68.

Want to know that vital question? Work it out.

The important question is hidden in this block of letters. All you have to do is to cross out every B, J, K, L, M, P, Q, V, W, X and Z to reveal the question. Simple!

```
B B K L X J Z Q P X
Z Q X A K Z R E V Y
X J B X M P K K V V
K Q O K U J T P Q B
L J V B H E C M H M
R K B I V S M P T T
W H E V W S Z J O K
L V L B J L B M X P
K N M J P O L V F M
L Q K G V K O V L D
```

Write the question in the question mark.

29

Jesus is tried by the Roman governor

The next morning, Jesus was put in chains and taken to Pilate, the Roman governor. He had the power of life and death over Jewish criminals. Pilate wasn't very impressed with the high priest's case.

"Are you the King of the Jews?" he asked. Again Jesus answered, "You have said so."

The crowd began to roar. I realised that the very people who last week had welcomed Jesus into Jerusalem had now turned against him. The crowd was crying out for Jesus to be killed. Pilate tried once more.

There's a Passover custom for the governor to release one prisoner. Pilate asked, "Shall I release Jesus of Nazareth?"

"No!" screamed the people. "Crucify him! Release Barabbas instead!" Barabbas was a convicted murderer.

Barabbas was a real thug who deserved to be punished. Can you find his name in this grid? Search across, down and diagonally up and down, left and right. The name only occurs once.

A	B	B	R	A	S	B	B
B	A	B	A	B	B	A	A
A	B	A	A	R	R	B	R
R	B	S	A	A	R	B	R
R	A	A	B	A	R	R	A
A	S	B	B	A	B	A	B
B	A	A	R	A	B	S	A
S	A	S	S	A	R	A	B

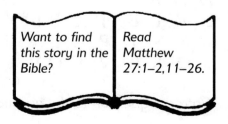

Want to find this story in the Bible? Read Matthew 27:1–2, 11–26.

30

Jesus is crucified

I followed the soldiers as they dragged Jesus through the streets, mocking and beating him as they went. Because he'd said he was "King of the Jews", someone made a circle of thorns and rammed it cruelly onto his head, like a crown. He was made to drag a heavy wooden cross towards the hill called Golgotha. Jesus kept stumbling so, after a while, a man from the crowd was forced to carry the cross instead.

Then the soldiers hammered nails into his hands and feet. Two thieves were crucified at the same time. The soldiers pulled the three crosses upright, Jesus in the middle. A massive crowd had gathered. Some people stared. Others wept. Jesus' mother was there with some other women and the eleven special friends.

The sky was dark as Jesus hung there till mid-afternoon. Suddenly the ground shook and the huge curtain in the temple was torn in half at that very moment. Then Jesus died.

While Jesus was on the cross, he spoke several times. Look on the next page to find out what he said.

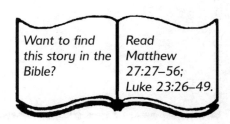

| Want to find this story in the Bible? | Read Matthew 27:27–56; Luke 23:26–49. |

This isn't exactly a puzzle. They're words to reflect on. That's the clue.

Father, forgive them for they do not know what they are doing.

I tell you the truth; today you will be with me in paradise.

Father, into your hands I commend my spirit.

31

Jesus is buried - and comes alive again!

The following day was the Sabbath, so the bodies had to be buried quickly. A man called Joseph, from Arimathea, asked for the body of Jesus.

Pilate said he could take the body, so Joseph laid Jesus in his own tomb. He rolled a huge stone over the entrance. Soldiers were set to guard the tomb because the Jewish leaders were afraid that some of us would steal the body.

The Sabbath passed and early on Sunday morning, some women who were friends of Jesus went to the tomb. They were hoping to put sweet smelling spices on Jesus' body. To their amazement, the heavy stone had been rolled away. The body had disappeared! The first we knew of it was when one of the women, Mary Magdalene, rushed back into town, shouting for Simon Peter to come. He and John ran to look. Mary returned to the tomb, sobbing because she thought someone had stolen Jesus' body. She saw a man she thought was the gardener. When he spoke to her, she realised this was Jesus himself!

Jesus was alive again, just as he'd promised!

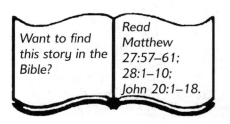

| Want to find this story in the Bible? | Read Matthew 27:57–61; 28:1–10; John 20:1–18. |

How many differences can you find?

32

Jesus goes back to heaven

Jesus stayed on earth for 40 days. He met lots of people and spoke about the kingdom of God. He said that soon his disciples would be given a special gift – the Holy Spirit. Jesus told his friends to go into every country to find new believers.

"Teach them everything I've taught you," he said, "and baptise them in the name of the Father and the Son and the Holy Spirit."

One day in Bethany, Jesus raised his arms, blessed his friends and went up into heaven! Soon a cloud hid him so that they could not see him any longer. He had gone to God his Father, just as he'd said he would.

As the eleven stood there, open-mouthed with astonishment, two men in white robes suddenly appeared. I suppose they must have been angels! What they said filled the friends of Jesus with joy. Find out by solving this puzzle – the last one!

Put a circle round the correct word and cross out the incorrect.

Why do you stand/sit here/there looking into the sky/sea? This same Jesus, who has been taken from you into home/heaven, will come back/front in the same day/way you have seen him no/go into heaven.

Write the angels' words in the cloud.

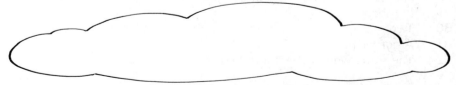

Want to find this story in the Bible? Read Matthew 28:19–20; Luke 24:50–53; Acts 1:7–11.

ANSWERS

Quiz

1 A dove (the Holy Spirit).
2 Honour.
3 Andrew and Simon.
4 Fishers of men.
5 Six.
6 Simon Peter.
7 Told everybody about Jesus.
8 Pick up his mat and walk.
9 In the synagogue.
10 Alphaeus.
11 They shall see God.
12 The kingdom of God.
13 The kingdom of heaven.
14 A camel.
15 His servant was ill.
16 To prepare the way.
17 Herodias.
18 5,000.
19 Bartimaeus.
20 Ephraim.
21 Cloaks and branches.
22 A den of robbers.
23 Our neighbour.
24 The Passover.
25 30 silver coins.
26 Bread and wine.
27 Simon Peter.
28 Are you the Christ, the Son of God?
29 Barabbas.
30 Two.
31 A gardener.
32 The same way he went into heaven.

Puzzles

1. The Holy Spirit came down like a dove on Jesus and a voice from heaven said, "This is my beloved Son. I am well pleased with him!"

2. "A prophet is often without honour in his own house and in his own country. He is not acceptable in his own land."

3. Andrew and Simon.

4. "Follow me and I will make you fishers of men."

5. Pieces 5, 6 and 9 do not belong to the jigsaw.

6. Simon Peter's mother-in-law had a fever. Jesus cured her. He took hold of her hand. The fever left her.

7. *Please see illustration.*

8. "Your sins are forgiven. Pick up your mat and go home." The man stood up, picked up his mat and walked away.

9. Pharisee 3 and 8 are the same.

10.

The remaining letters spell the sentence, "Jesus calls the twelve disciples."

61

11 "Blessed are the poor in spirit, for theirs is the kingdom of heaven.
Blessed are the meek, for they shall inherit the earth.
Blessed are the merciful, for they shall receive mercy.
Blessed are the pure in heart, for they shall see God."

12 "Seek first the kingdom of God."

13 "Let the little children come to me. Do not try to hinder them for
the kingdom of heaven belongs to such as these."

14 "It is easier for a camel to go through the eye of a needle than for
a rich man to enter the kingdom of God."

15 Roman: "Lord, my servant is at home, very ill."
Jesus: "I will go and heal him."
Roman: "Just say the word and my servant will be healed."
Jesus: "I have not found anyone in Israel with such great faith."

16 "I say there is no greater prophet than John the Baptist."

17 Herod had married his brother's wife, Herodias. John said that this
was wrong. Herodias was angry and with the help of her daughter
Salome, tricked Herod into promising to kill John.

18

Sum 1		Sum 2	
Crowd	5,000	Crowd	4,000
Loaves	5	Days there	3
Fish	2	Loaves	7
Baskets of leftovers	12	Baskets of leftovers	7
	5,019		4,017

5,019 — 4,017 = 1,002

19 Blind, apostles, rowing, Tyre, Iscariot, Mary, Andrew, Exodus,
Unleavened, Sabbath. The initial letters spell "Bartimaeus".

20 Ephraim.

21 *Please see illustration.*

22 "It is written 'My house will be called a house of prayer.' But you are making it a den of robbers!"

23 The first great commandment is, "You shall love the Lord your God with all your heart, with all your soul and with all your mind." The second is, "You shall love your neighbour as yourself."

24 "In two days it will be the Passover festival and the Son of Man will be handed over to be crucified."

25 Judas Iscariot arranged to betray Jesus for thirty silver coins.

26 "I am the way, the truth, the life."

27 All the disciples except Simon Peter ran away.

28 "Are you the Christ, the Son of God?"

29 The name Barabbas runs from top right corner to bottom left corner.

30 "Father, forgive them, for they do not know what they are doing." "I tell you the truth; today you will be with me in paradise." "Father, into your hands I commend my spirit."

31 *Please see illustration.*

32 "Why do you stand here looking into the sky? This same Jesus, who has been taken from you into heaven, will come back in the same way you have seen him go into heaven."

If you want to know more about becoming a follower of Jesus, you can read…

Me +Jesus and *Jesus=Friendship forever* are booklets to help you when you decide to become one of Jesus' friends. Easy to read, with zany pictures, they cost 99p each.

If you enjoyed reading your Bible, why not read a bit every day? *Snapshots* is a booklet to help adventurers like you to hear God's message to you as you read the Bible. Full of fun, puzzles and prayer ideas, it comes out every three months. £2.50.

10 Rulz will give you a whole new way of looking at Moses and the Ten Commandments – cartoons that will make you laugh and stories about some of the horrible things people in the Bible shouldn't have done to each other! £4.99.

Prices correct at the time of going to print.